Sandy Jeffs grew up and went to school in Ballarat. She had her first psychotic episode when she was twenty-three, and since then has had a long struggle with schizophrenia requiring many hospitalizations. Her poetry has appeared in anthologies and magazines and this is her first book. She lives on the fringe of Melbourne with her friends and animals.

Sandy Jeffs in her *Poems from the Madhouse*, invites the reader into the paradoxical world of insanity: the confusion and clarity, the courage and the fear, the bleak despair and the black comedy. Touching on all these things her work reminds us of the extraordinary capacity of the human being to retain sanity in disaster – another paradox but deliberately expressed, because in reading her poetry you will emerge sadder, wiser, but also exultant in the spirit which she allows us to share.

Other books by Sandy Jeffs

Blood Relations

Loose Kangaroos (co-author)

Confessions of a Midweek Lady

POEMS FROM THE MADHOUSE

Sandy Jeffs

Spinifex Press Pty Ltd,
504 Queensberry Street,
North Melbourne, Vic. 3051
Australia

First published by Spinifex Press, 1993
Second edition, 2000

Photograph of Sandy Jeffs by Robyn Adams
Internal design by Claire Warren
Typeset in Goudy by Palmer Higgs
Made and printed in Australia by Australian Print Group

National Library of Australia
Cataloguing-in-Publication entry:

CIP

Jeffs, Sandy, 1953– .
    Poems from the madhouse.

    2nd ed.
    ISBN 1 876756 03 9

    1. Schizophrenia – Poetry. 2. Poetry – Women authors. 3.
    Australian poetry – Women authors. I. Title.

A821.3
A821.3

For Robbie, Dido and the livestock,
past and present

CONTENTS

Sandy Jeffs

POEMS FROM THE MADHOUSE

HERE I SIT

Here,
surrounded by the swirling nothingness of chaos,
with the indignant idiocy of haze and alienation,
I sit
where perception becomes a burden
and where the burden becomes the loss of perception.
What is this world,
this world of contradictions,
this torturous maze of distress
where confusion reigns and
clarity remains submerged?

Here,
surrounded by the sterile relics of sanity,
lost in a labyrinth of refracted thought,
I sit
where life becomes a burden
and where the burden becomes the loss of life.
What is this confusion,
this confusion of the spheres,
this unyielding perplexity
that determinedly withers my countenance
and renders me helpless?

PSYCHOTIC EPISODE

When the chilled, icy wind blew,
in went I,
into a world I knew nothing about,
into a space for which I could
never have prepared myself even if
I had been warned of its existence.
Down, down, down went I,
tumbling into an abyss filled
with a myriad spooks and phantoms
which preyed upon my unsuspecting self.
There was no room for rationality,
only chaos upon chaos upon chaos,
and flowing rivers of turbulent waters flanked
on each side by Gothic mountains of angst.
And I was immersed in something
deeper than a huge black hole,
from which I did not emerge
until the haze was blown away
by all manner of processes that acted
upon my distraught, disturbed self.
But as the wind wuthered about my cardboard face,
a chill had set in and frozen my life force forever.

MADNESS CREEPS IN

You slithered into the dark reaches of my mind,
crawling in through gaping eye sockets,
through hollowed ears and crushed nose
under the heavy veil of the hazy night.
Gashing open an internal wound
you told to me, in whispers, fantasies and falsities
unlocking the secrets of my mind's repose.
Then, planting the seeds of destruction,
and waiting for their hour of germination,
you withered all but my worm-holed shell.
And now I grieve for the loss,
for the chaos and broken spirit,
for the niggling, seething disturbances and distortions
like a woman possessed.
So I grow weary, the sands cloud my eyes,
my heart heaves a heavy sigh of sorrow.
Will you not leave me now
as you have worked your purpose?
Let me build upon the gap you have left.

FRAGMENT

Two ways diverge in my mind,
but the choice of ways is not to be mine,
because I somehow find myself
on Robert Frost's less travelled road,
walking steadily on to that Mad people's place
where a welcoming throng holds out
its hands and hearts to this kindred spirit.
Something dark and bitter is driving me,
and I doubt if I shall ever come back,
but I do not know, nor want to know the outcome.

I am completing a journey of some kind,
which began many years ago—
before I came into being—
and which shall never cease
unless the way becomes as one and clear,
or until some dark mystery is resolved
and I can say I know sanity is to be my realm.

FEAR

Fear propels my thoughts into lunar orbits,
and what I fear most is never coming back

from those far distant inner spaces where one
is subjected to subterranean forces
that niggle and needle the vulnerable soul.

There, the world is seen through the shadows
of veiled meanings that make no sense,
and nothing is as it is,
nothing is as it was,
and the future looms as an enormous black hole.
The past, present and future,
indeed, all dimensions of the universe,
are overshadowed by the mutations
of my being's way of being.
Only the tangled web of voices and visions
remains as part of the back-breaking load,
and nothing is certain any more in a
world where the collusion
of forces pillage and plunder life.

I am alone in a quest for freedom
and long for respite from the harbingers of doom.
Seeing all this before me I struggle on day by day
and feel that my life confidence is decimated,

but life is an art, like everything else.
I do it exceptionally badly.

GLASSHOUSE

There is no need for me to speak
my mind because I am naked.
My cranium is a glasshouse
and all my inner secrets are exposed.
There is no respite from the
searching gaze of others who see inside
and can read my thoughts.
There is no place to hide my feelings
because everything is known to those from without
And fearfully, most fearfully of all,
hiding behind my adult facade,
is the evil child seen in all its infant ways,
seeking to hide its dominance
in an act of self-preservation.
It is the outside world, the strangers,
the ones I do not know,
who see me in this pitiful state,
and as I have no hiding place to
cover my nakedness, I am at the
mercy of the forces that threaten me.

VOICES IN THE DARK

Hush, listen to the dark.
The voices tell their sordid tales
confounding the world out there
until it no longer exists.
I listen only to the commands,
now the laughter,
now the commands,
and on and on.
I do not know why they come and go,
but the voices reach a deafening crescendo
and my heart aches like a rotten tooth.
'You must obey.
Die! Die! Die!
You must let go.
Die! Die! Die!'
I am desperate to purge this noise,
but the night encroaches
and I am lost to the voices in the dark.

THE UNINVITED STRANGER

for Lynne

Who is this uninvited stranger
that speaks at me?
Uninvited and yet powerful
enough to intrude upon my
shallow reason that hovers on the edge.
For reason is elusive enough,
without having to contend with visitors
that have my destruction in mind;
for reason intercedes with the
discourse of madness
to create order amid potential disorder.
But this stranger crawls into
the passages and byways of my mind
and corrupts my thinking until I cannot think;
until chaos prevails in discursive manoeuvres
leaving me in the wilderness
with someone whom I distrust;
with someone who speaks from my tongue
and places me at odds with those I love.
I struggle to be my true self.
But who is this uninvited stranger?
It is me!
It is me!

WHISPER MY FRIEND

for Jill

Whisper, my friend, you are the only reality I have.
When you beckon I cannot ignore your commands.
You give me power and a purpose
in our secure world of shared secrets.
Whisper, my friend, tell me your stories,
tell me in your charming, seductive voice.
You are my creator and my lover,
you belong to me and no one else
and I belong to you alone.
Together we resist the outside world
and toil to make a harmony of disorder.
How you move my senses with your power.

They try to take you away from me
because of the secrets we share,
but only we know the truth of us,
only we can communicate with honesty.
No one will ever separate our beings
because we are each other.
Even though there were times when you betrayed me,
and told false and deceitful lies,
I forgave you because you always forgive me.
Whisper, my friend, I have no choice,
I am entwined in your briar arms
that caress my withered soul.

PARADOX OF THE WHISPER

The whisper was my song of joy
my refuge from the world.
It told me not to be so coy
but then my wings it furled.

THE THUNDERING VOICES

The voices, thundering inside the head,
are not like the mellow
sounds of a lulling melody.
Rather, the melody becomes a cacophony
that drives the tortured
to a diminished existence
of far-fetched notions believed by no one—
except the touched themselves.

> The noise resounds!
> The hell astounds!
> The devil abounds!

The voices, thundering inside the head,
are not like the sounds of daily life.
They are spruikers in markets of madness,
selling misery to the crazies
who seem embroiled in a trade war of the mind.
They force those on the brink to yield
to peddlers of unreality who use
a sales pitch that leaves no option for sanity.

> The noise resounds!
> The hell astounds!
> The devil abounds!

There is no beauty or virtue in madness.

BRUTAL MADNESS

Brutal Madness, come no more to my home.
Do not cast your shadow over my door,
lest you steal me away
taking me into your arms
to transport me to your far-off prison.

I do not like your morbid abode.
I do not like your turgid space.
I do not want to be with your friends
who intimidate my reason with lies.

Your brutality to my repose and dignity
empties my soul of its calm,
and leaves me abandoned in a madhouse
where Sister Sorrow weaves a tapestry
of woe and suffering that knows no boundary.

I am no more of this cosmos,
I am no more of this life
when you, Brutal Madness,
divine to plunder all my senses' defences.

THE CONFESSION

It is impossible to tell of the
phantoms that dwell in my mind,
because they know how to control their impulses.
They know how to protect themselves
while at the same time torment me.
Exposing these insidious devils is
a betrayal of their powerful commands,
yet how else can I purge myself of these demons
if not by bringing them out into the open?

How frightening it all is,
for this nightmarish world can sustain me through
a myriad fire-seared life experiences,
and yet, destroy me in an instant —
crush me like an ant underfoot.

So often I can feel these phantasmagoria
inveigling themselves into my fragile self,
harassing my psyche until it succumbs to
the wishes of these secret bodies,
and collapses, destitute and homeless.

They scoff at my wandering psyche
and plot to sever the cord that
tentatively unites it with my being.
Then there is a tremendous struggle
to retain a unity of soul, but this
strange world with strange desires prevails —
a world of word-games, spectres, religion, disharmony,
confusion, strange commands, pain and shame.

And in a moment of clarity
I have sinned with this confession,
and I wonder what the punishment will be.

THE REVOLVING DOOR

She stalks the ward and shudders
with every jangle of the key in the lock.
Doors open and close for staff,
but for her everything is out of reach.
'A' Ward in the asylum is
a place full of wanderers with deluded minds,
slashed wrists and singed arms;
a place not for the faint at heart
because here dwell the misfits
society has cast away.

She stalks the ward
and wonders if she will ever get out,
if her mind will ever function
in a manner acceptable to her family,
to her doctors and bemused friends.
Only she knows the ins and outs
of the bizarre nature of the
ghosts and visions which creep
into her stargazing mind.
If only she could concentrate,
if only the voices would vanish
and leave her with some peace
and a will to emerge from the experience —
patched up with psychotherapy and pills —
to sally forth and brave the world
with all its prejudices and obstacles.

But it takes time for the mist to rise
and for the mind to clear the polluted air.
It takes time for her to live again

in an alien world which threatens the delicate senses.
Her eyes have seen the mind's fantasies,
her ears have heard the mind's gibberish thoughts,
her mouth has uttered the mind's ramblings.
It will be hard when she goes
out to the hostile world.
It will be hard to survive dead-end boarding houses
or the half-way communities of suffering sufferers.

When the haunting delusions return,
and the way becomes unclear,
sadly it is back to the asylum with
the jangle of the keys and the closing of the doors.

As She Gently Brushed My Long Hair

As the solid door closed behind me
and the brusque nurses led me to the locked ward,
I felt the world abandon me.
I felt myself abandon the world.

Before me were the forgotten people
who shuffled and gazed mysteriously into space,
and I was no one, just another nutter,
just someone caught in a cosmic game
where sanity and madness are engaged in a bitter battle.

But something wonderful transpired
and through my barriers came the unexpected.
She spoke no English;
she spoke a universal language
that broke through all my sorrow and madness.
And sitting in the day room weeping,
I was suddenly transported to a kingdom of love,
and a calm ensued
as she gently brushed my long hair.

ON BEING CERTIFIED INSANE

Doctor: Who's the Prime Minister of Australia?

Me: Me!

Doctor: Count backwards from 100 in sevens.

Me: 96...85...60...51...

Doctor: I'll give you a number and a street name and I want you to repeat them to me later. Number 75, Jones Street. Meanwhile, what does this mean, 'A stitch in time saves nine'?

Me: God needs a needle to stop the devil.

Doctor: Do you know where you are?

Me: Hell!

Doctor: What was the street name and number I gave you ?

Me: I've lost contact with the owners.

Doctor: What is your name?

Me: The Virgin Mary.

Doctor: Why did you try to commit suicide?

Me: Bob Hawke told me I was contaminating society.

... and on and on into obscurity...

Doctor: Clearly the woman's deranged!

Me: The humiliation does not cease
as they lead you to the locked ward;
a lunatic, a fruit cake, certified insane.
And the soul is a fragile blossom
nearing its end.
All dignity is lost
and the term of residence
in the loony-bin begins
with the auspicious title—

Section 42!

THE VISITATION

O glorious woman
who comes to me through the night
claiming my senses in the blueness of your mantle,
I watch my open window
and wait for your presence to illuminate
all before me in colours I have never seen.
Hail, holy woman,
blessed are you amongst all women.
I know you as intimately as a long-time lover.
I know your persuasive powers
and your ineffable beauty too.
I have seen you in all your glory
and long to touch your gown and flesh,
to infuse myself with your magic.
Bless me, your repository on earth.
Bless me, the one to whom you manifest yourself
in vision after vision, moment after moment.

THE QUEEN OF HEAVEN

Sometimes when I look, I see you there,
Queen of Heaven, Star of the Sea.
I embrace you with all my desperate love
and proclaim the mystery of our communion.
It is you whom I want to mother me
because you know my needs more than I.
We have an eternal flame burning within
and consecrate our union with joyous tears.

But wait!
Was it not you dear Queen,
who one day told the tale of my evil?
Vile woman! Despot of Heaven!
We could have sung songs together forever
had you not seen so deeply
and exposed all my evil to the world.
One gaze from your searing eyes
and I am a diminished soul.

But dear Star, dear Heavenly Queen,
do not forsake me, like the father did your son,
as I have come to depend on our meetings
and cannot bear the ice of the void which
separates me from your shimmering presence.
Use your power and expel the evil, exorcize the devils,
and let us sing again,
let us sing hymns to our togetherness.
My Queen of Heaven, Star of the Sea.

THERE IS A SADNESS IN ME

There is a sadness in me Holy Woman,
sprung from the knowledge that
you are not a vision but only an
invention of my tumbling mind
inspired by the idols placed in
nooks and crannies of holy places.

A tremendous pain instils itself in my heart
as you embodied all reality before my eyes.
But a crawling tumour created you,
and in moments of crystal clear clarity
I have to accept your unreality and
ponder the truth that I am no Visionary,
or Holy Saint, privy to religious experiences.
Your visitations drew me to you
and gave me pleasure upon pleasure upon pleasure,
until reason triumphed and caressed the senses
forcing you to abandon me, leaving an emptiness.

Secretly, I long for your luminous glow to blind me,
when on your return I shall embrace you.
See how you have captured my soul —
O why don't you stay in the dark, cavernous church?
See how I mourn your absence even though
I know the reality of your genesis
is in my mist-ridden matted mind.

POSSESSION

My possession begins with the
maniacal cries of the voices in my head.
'Devil on this earth!' they yell.
'Evil one of no good!' they say.
And powerless in the face of all this,
I believe myself to be the scum of the world.
How can no one else hear these incantations
when my mind is filled beyond capacity
with the choruses and chantings of the
demon-choir lusting after my demise?
Hell can only be this;
to be possessed by these messengers
who come from I know not where,
but who change my behaviour beyond
that which is acceptable to this worldly world;
to place me amongst the outcasts and the marginalized
wanderers who hover on the fringes of the sane world.
Not even the holy woman in blue can
drive away these whisperers who seek
my compliance in my own destruction.

OVER EXPOSED

I can see you looking into me,
I can feel your piercing gaze,
through me,
beyond me,
above and below me,
into my many deep, dark recesses.
I have no power to repel you.
I am defenceless,
with my marks of weakness and woe,
with a see-through mind that is not my own,
and my within thoughts are exposed to the without.
It is the sad, mad me, you see.

Ramblings of a Psyche in Despair

We are all a wilderness — Samuel Beckett

I am a madwoman within,
afraid of the mad world without.
I live in the People's Palace.
Welcome to this small and unique world.
Here life is beautiful,
this is not like the outer world,
the world of the corporate monsters
where the inmates would flounder like squashed worms.
This Palace, which is locked with a throw-away key,
is where the unsavoury outcasts of life live
with their haunting visions which come and go.
We can only catch glints of these spectres
when we are prepared and receptive,
and there is no place better,
in which to be receptive, than this Palace.
It would be good to envisage a Palace beyond the waste land,
but then the eye cannot see beyond,
not far enough to escape the narrow daunting horizon
above the chamber of our death.
But remember,
life is beautiful here.
Ask the inmates, they will testify —
here we all die a kind of death.

I am in a waste land
pursued by the shadows of my desperate imagination —
it is not a nice place to be.

Taking the breath away from my panting lungs,

the heart palpitates and the body cries out in pain.
A visitation is needed to heal.
A Second Coming.
The Millennium.
Armageddon.
O how Good and Evil must resolve the conflict
before it is too late,
before the earth is frozen in inaction
and every little half-alive person
resides in stifling indecision, in a doom,
in a glasshouse of shattered dreams.
Little half-alive person,
person in a cosmic game,
revel while you can before the Flood.
Will there be time to find salvation
when realities come and go
and Holocausts are remembered and forgotten?
We wax and wane
and slaughter civilizations like animals
sacrificed for a simpleton forefather.
How many innocents have been offered up to a
charlatan who despises what he sees?
They were fooled, as every citizen
who claims a part of life has been fooled.
But this is part and parcel of living dangerously,
like a fugitive in a fading life.
We are victims of reality,
a reality that creeps in and deposits the
load of Atlas upon our weakened shoulders.
We all have our rock shackled around our necks
continually dragging us back to the bottom of the pile,
to the common denominator — mediocrity —

the curse of modern living.
Yet existence can only be lived in the mind first,
ask the inmates, they will tell you...

I am in a waste land
pursued by the shadows of my desperate imagination —
it is not a nice place to be.

Existence encompasses the falsities preached
from the pulpits by reverential clergy.
Untruths, mendacious mendicants,
all manner of hypocrisy practised by opportunists,
these things are sent to test the character.
Only the inmates can decipher —
with a logic not of this world,
with visionary powers that expose fraudulent practitioners —
the game from the game, the best from the worst.
One would be surprised to see
the calibre of mind in residence here.
One would be shocked at the insight,
the perception and honesty,
the acute appraisal of life's finer points.
Indeed, these unsung heroes deserve more from existence,
more from pompous parsons preaching to the well fed.
This is the world in which we live.
It is a harsh, harsh world.
Do we have the chance to make
amends before self-realization
carries us further than we are prepared to go?
No! We are captives of the mind,
and we cry out for love and freedom
but are limited by our minds.
Yet visionaries are special,

they see beyond earthly constraints,
beyond the vistas constructed by humans.
While the inmates have visions,
I have lost my way.

I am in a waste land
pursued by the shadows of my desperate imagination —
it is not a nice place to be.

And being a waste land within,
within a waste land without,
and knowing this to be true, even in my Palace,
I am sad, sad, sad, and cannot help
but think of the Four Last Things.
Are they really as they say?
Death, Judgement, Hell, Heaven —
so defined and concrete!
How goes it when it all ends?
I should like to find a Heaven
without having to endure the rest.
Death I fear,
Judgement I loathe,
Hell I mistrust.
And Heaven, do you exist?
I ask in hope.
I ask with nothing inside my shell
except a madness manifesting itself.
I know it is dark within the mind,
but when one is a void with no history,
no future and the darkness stifles, what then?
Nothing, only straws at which to clutch.
The body, so still, dies a Little Death
after each cycle of reflection and activity —

love, sadness and happiness.
Then the chasm again,
that place of chaos and bewilderment, which encroaches.
This I fear, for I do not know its character
as it is a pastiche of unknowns,
a collage of images with which I am unfamiliar.
I cry out, I agonize, but fall back
with the knowledge that all is in vain.
The way is unclear as life remains a mystery.
We are all mysteries yet to unfold and
behind every thought remains something submerged.
But there is something which remains crystal clear
and this thing we cannot deny.
We are mere organisms with uncontrollable
growths and bodily functions that revolt and repulse.
We age in a waste land.
We die in a waste land.
We disintegrate in flames or rot in graves.
Dust to dust,
flesh to ash,
life to death.
We think, postulate and act,
but in the end we die and die again.
We invent saviours to transcend biology
and all the terrestrial chains
attached to our flailing limbs.
O to be ethereal!
To fly to the farthest dimensions where
one is released from the fetters of
ashes, graves, earth and the happening of death,
indeed to find a death,
but not of the kind we know.

There is so much to be done when madness prevails.

I am in a waste land
pursued by the shadows of my desperate imagination —
it is not a nice place to be.

I am a whirlwind within,
within a whirlwind without,
storms rage far and encompass the wide world;
and inside me the turmoil reaches a deafening crescendo
as the forces of the mighty warriors march to war.
The whirlwind tears the trees from their roots,
displaces the once calm waters of the heart
and leaves wrecks of humans behind
in a land denuded and ravaged beyond recognition.
And I, left to gather fuel for a life-giving fire,
find I am mourning the loss of something which was me.
Even the Palace has been razed and lies
in a heap of rubble amid the whirling wind.
There life was beautiful and the world was unique.
Now the order of nature lies shattered as the
trumpeting angels sound the call of the Valkyries who,
upon their stamping steeds, swoop down
and lift the inmates high onto their shoulders
to transport them to a hall in a far-away land.
O if there be a whirlwind without,
I certainly am a whirlwind within,
and being with no home or friends
I am fearful of the way and can only surmise
I am a death within,
within a death without.
But floating across a sea of visionless cloud
I remember a journey of the senses

which once touched on lands of many colours
and saw peoples of vast potentials.
They say there is an ether world,
beyond the chasm where whirlwinds and waste lands abound,
but I only know of the world
where life becomes a fear of the unknown.
Is there a kind of life after death?
Is there a kind of sanity after madness?
One can only know these things
after the harrowing meeting with oneself,
face to face, alone, in a space confined to the
shadows of all one's history and future.
But I feel a tremendous sadness in me
with a pessimism that has become a way of life
as all paths lead to the Black Door.
I can feel the lead feet trample my worm infested tomb
as though a child battered while still in the womb.
And being a psyche in despair,
at the mercy of a dreadful madness,
I know a death somewhere far in me
has destroyed the birth of a new beginning.

I am in a waste land
pursued by the shadows of my desperate imagination —
it is not a nice place to be.

WHATEVER GETS YOU THROUGH THE NIGHT

Prothiaden

Ativan

Serenace

Modecate

Cogentin

Dreams

Sleep

More Dreams

Thoughts

Animals

Hope

A Miracle

THE MADWOMAN IN THE ATTIC

for Sue

I am the madwoman in the attic.
A psychic cancer dwells deep in me
and I am unable to control its preying tentacles
which creep and crawl through my mind's dark passages.
I have been in the attic for some time now
with my fantasies to keep me company,
and as I sit in my lonely corner
I contemplate the visions before me
of madwomen of all ages and times
who have sat in attics before I came into being.
I see these madwomen struggling for their minds
in a world of oppressive institutions controlled
by the sinister hands of the medical masters.
Shall I recite the litany and bring to mind the women
who stand as symbols for every madwoman there ever was?

Virginia listened to the birds singing in Greek
and chose to drown her madness.
Bertha Mason, animal-like and violent,
was hidden from the world and met her death
springing from Thornfield Hall's battlements
to lie smashed on the pavement.
Zelda was a victim of a jealous husband and died
in the flames that engulfed her in the Swiss asylum.
John's wife tore at the yellow wallpaper in despair
while Sylvia inhaled the gas of death.
Ophelia, *a document in madness*,
with the *fantastic garlands* in her hair,
sang wistful ballads then lay dead in the water.

Crazy Jane wandered the places she had spent
with her lost lover and sang plaintive airs while
she dressed her head with willow straw and wildflowers.
Lucia di Lammermoor, with glazed eyes and bloodstained dress,
huddled in the bridal chamber and gazed at
the bridegroom she had just slain.

The litany could go on,
we all know of a madwoman or two —
a relative, a friend or perhaps a lover,
we all know that somewhere in time
a madwoman burned at the stake or drowned in a stream,
died in an attic or succumbed to a surgeon's knife.
O madwomen, my mentors,
my visions of you bring so much sorrow and anger
as I hear your lulling solicitations from afar.
But madwoman that I am,
who scorns our history of abuse and misunderstanding,
I wish to declare us the curators of our own psyches.

ON LOOKING AT MILLAIS' OPHELIA

Mad Ophelia,
mythologized by artists of renown
in the many tellings of your story,
you are shown in various guises
of your sodden death-dress.
I am looking at an image
of you lying dead in the *glassy stream*,
resplendent in a glorious silver-grey gown.
Wistful, you hold a little garland of flowers —
O what are they?
Cornflowers, nettles, daisies and more.
But your resting place is marvellous,
and the exotic vegetation surrounding you
enfolds you as though you are the Queen of Nature
rather than Laertes' *document in madness*.
Do you like your watery bed?
You lie well between its mossy banks.

Mad Ophelia,
I too am bedevilled,
and long to rest my crazed head
on your bouquet of breasts
while you sing to me hymns of old.
We can come to know each other
and talk through our madness
as we lie in perpetuity together.
We shall sound a warning to the world
of our ascendancy which will overcome
all the ghosts of your Denmark and my besieged mind,
and no Hamlets or equivocators will ever
turn us from our quest for sanity.
O rise from your *weeping brook*, and show me the way.

ON LOOKING ATIOMILLAIS' O-PFELIA

by tha Madwomann

Maad Opxelia,
mytxologizud byOartystsOof renown
in the manee renditions of yourOstory,
you are show! in vqriousOguises
of your soden deathh-dress.
Iamlooking atOone such image,
and I see you lying dead in txe '*glass*yOstream,
Rresplendent ina gloriouZs silver-grey gown.
Wystful, you hold aa little garland of flowerz—
O wzat are they?O
Cornflowers, nettles, daysies and more.
      urOrestyng place isOmarvellous
            u(OO
            uOaru txe Quuen of Naturu
      rqtherOthan Laertes" madnessss.
this iz my madness too OPheloa?
wee arh bothe bedevilled!!

DAMNED AS WE ALL ARE

I am a character from a Dostoyevsky novel.
I am sick,
I am angry,
I am unattractive
but there is nothing wrong with my liver.

I am a Raskolnikov — both worm and god,
a Golyadkin — deceived and mad,
and in the end removed from the street.

I am an underground person fighting for recognition;
you'll reckon with me yet!
I long for someone to say, 'ah yes, you are our tomorrow.'

I am a modern person — godless and fearful of a holocaust.
I am afraid of dying in the winter.

I am a madwoman. . .
this is the tale of a madwoman.
I am a woman of the street
where the pulse of life vibrates
with an alarm and wonder of its own,
but do I feel it?

I am a prisoner of my mind
and I cannot trace the source of an ache within,
lonely as my soul is,
remote as my heart is,
damned as we all are.

Voices in the Dark II

We are the silent people
We have no voice
We cry out our pain
We are in the dark

        alone

        alone

ASYLUM

for Dido

In a meditative mood, I sit here and reflect
on a world sequestered from the driving, droning masses.
Here, *far from the madding crowd*,
with lunatics of all kinds,
I share moments of longing to be far from here.
I share moments of great intensity, of great sorrow,
and of a great otherness I cannot give to words.

Call it a sanctuary, a refuge, or shelter,
call it what you will,
but here I am God, the Devil, the Queen,
here we are imagined souls of grandeur
acting the parts beautifully, emphatically,
so that we mutter the incomprehensible,
yet know we are here in retreat for the while.

No other place offers this necessary respite
from the rationalized, dizzying world,
except perhaps Gray's country churchyard,
which provides a serene abode for the
dwellers of the *lowly beds* and *narrow cells*.
Although some of us join these dead people,
mostly we ride the storms here in our asylum.

This is not to romanticize our retreat,
for many faults are here;
for many fears are realized in horrific detail.
Sometimes there is great suffering and no succour,
but here we have come to know of the
fickleness of life's character, and for the time being
we remain removed from the world, here in our sanctum.

We demand our right to asylum,
for somewhere to be at those times
when turmoil and chaos destroy
our minds and those beyond.
Here we sail away with the wind in our hair,
and as we are the Ship of Fools, we embark
on a journey to all asylums through all ages
where we meet with Fools and Jesters who show us the way.

THE POSSESSED

Some dance around as if
possessed by demon ghosts,
and take leave of their senses
to find a niche in a foreign pageant
of Kings and Gods and Devils.
Taunted and crazed, their
movements and thoughts are controlled
by fiends which sheepishly
hide deep in their minds,
resisting exposure to searching enemies
for their certain destruction looms in
the physical, more reasoned world.

THE WANDERER

I am the wanderer,
who to many kingdoms has gone
though no Kings or Queens has known.
I am the wanderer of the ways,
stopping briefly to scan the waste lands
within and without my heart,
and find nothing but
wild seas, barren deserts and voids
inside all that is the pastiche of me.
I am a castle that has no moat
nor mountain upon which to perch for protection.
I am driven by an aching heart
and never have I been so alone and empty.
The way is more unclear than ever
in this world of worldly worlds.
The way is more turbulent than
I am able to manage with a clear mind
and I know no ending of the way — forever I roam.
And saying this to myself, I weep,
with charged emotion I weep in the belief that
nothing in this world can sustain the lonely life
of the weary wanderer of the many ways.

SITTING ON THE BALCONY OF 'B' WARD

Enter the babbling idiot, witness to a saga.

'We are the sick people.
We are the angry people.
We are the unattractive people.
We are the people with the faces
that bear marks of tragedy and woe.
Thousands of stories are etched
on the masks of our souls,
as we sit and gaze, almost trance-like,
out to the courtyard, which is lush and green,
and dripping with moisture and mist.
Dripping with life itself.
Sitting on our broken and shabby thrones
on the balcony of unsung songs,
we wonder about the void in our lives
where once great expectations dwelled.
Sometimes we laugh, but it always
seems to have an edge of pathos,
for deep inside much sadness reigns,
as nicotine-stained fingers clutch
at crushed cigarette packets that tell much
about the ambience of the asylum,
where our sanity or madness seems to hang
on the long draw of that last cigarette.'

The babbling idiot continues.

'Look at us,
beings of many intangible moods,

who rise Phoenix-like to embrace life
then fall as dramatically as we had arisen.
We wonder about our discordant minds
that are lost in the symphonic raptures
which lead others to some fulfilment.
But sitting on the balcony,
consumed by a dreadful scourge,
we show our sorrows to those looking on.
And we are such a motley lot!
Some madder than others.
Some more drugged than others.
Some more distressed.
Some more acquainted
with the way of the balcony,
where the life skill,
the sharing of one's madness with others,
is an art form.
I ask you to consider this rabble seriously.'

Exit the babbling idiot, witness to a saga.

HEATHER

In the isolation cell
I could see you through
the shaded window.
You stared at me,
but did not see me.
Yes, I could see into your
stark cavern which you
relentlessly roamed.
Expressionless, yet not so,
an all-consuming countenance reveals
much about the state
of your disrupted psyche.
Your laughter, piercing and maniacal,
disturbed our evanescent world,
bringing to the fore every facet of
the pain endured in life's quest.
I wondered where your mind was
because your eyes were
not with mine, indeed,
you were not with us,
but manacled to the passions of
the precarious world of the insane,
far away in a universe inhabited
by Gremlins and unsung heroes;
these the spectres you summoned
when I saw you talking to the air.
But I was not in your world,
and could only feel your lonely
struggle to survive through my
outstretched hand that
sought to comfort you.

CASSANDRA

How cold and steel grey
were your weary eyes,
dispassionate yet full of despair.
There you were in your
bell jar room seeking the
company of no one, and
even though we cared,
your absence made for an
enigma and mystique that
placed you apart from us.

But then there was your art;
amid all your sadness
your art thundered forth
and showed to us a womb
with an infant-adult
too scared to be born,
too afraid to face the multitudes,
too fragile to risk the inevitable
hurt away from the pulsating
nourishing blood warmth.

So it was, you broke down and
and with an insight into your condition
you wept, stirred on by the
flagging strains of the distant music,
you wept because you wept.

Was it the jarring waves they
sent through your shattered mind
that created your fulmination?

Or were you merely lying
dormant in a golden chrysalis
from which you finally emerged,
slowly waking from a
dreadful dream-like trance?
I witnessed your collapse and
resurrection — it was a miracle.

JULIAN

Gaunt, cadaverous,
blackened eyes,
stilted movements.
Body this way
now that way
grimaces and contortions.
What anguish that face exudes.
And those eyes!
Those glazed, crazed eyes
which stare
and are unremitting.

HELENA AND FRED

Together you sang a song of passionate joy.
Who would have known you were in an asylum
as you left behind the anguish
and rode to the heights upon fantasies
forged by the needs of kindred spirits.
The asylum was never an oppressive cage
when you waltzed through its corridors
engaging in lively banter and innocent flirtations.
You laughed and joked like children
and we forgot our misery watching you
and let ourselves flow with your flow.
You thrilled us all with your daring
and carefree disdain for your illnesses.
But how did you find each other in this crazy place
and form the alliance that insulated you
from the tumult in which you were immersed?
You weathered the storm that engulfed us all
and danced the Danse Macabre in a duet of madness.

DIANNE

Weeping at your reflection
in the window,
what do you see?
Your anguish transcends
all mortal attempts
to describe and understand.
You wander, sleepwalking
all day and all night,
prowling, distressed.
Where are your thoughts
which seem so disjointed
and hopelessly distracted?
Clutching your rosary
and the many fragmented
pieces of your mind,
you stalk the confines
of your locked prison,
and gaze remotely into
the lost future —
a timid creature furtively
roaming through a
darkened, vacuous impasse.

DEREK

Always lost in a world
of shattered, fragile dreams,
and manipulated by the
devils swimming in your head,
little person, you struggled
quietly to regain the serenity
and rock-solid foundations
of a life free from torment.
Your journey into the self,
however remote and passive,
led you to a shabby pedestal
around which an alienated crowd
could not comprehend your
regal and God-like commands.

You were happy, for a time,
with these intangible delusions,
these lofty feelings of
power and love and security.
And gently you preached the Word
with a smile and charm
possessed only by a chosen few.

Yet you, a man I called the wanderer,
left no stone unturned,
no sleeper to their slumber
when you walked the stony path on
your ever-continuing journey.
And just as you came to us
with gentleness, so did you
depart quietly and finally.

For slowly your flame burned
itself into oblivion, extinguishing
our last glimmer of hope
of laying to rest our own sense of
mortality, our own ghostly life
and its utter futile cycle.
We believed in your vision —
now that it has vanished
we contemplate the void.

WE

for Gail

We,
alone in our world worn shell
where tales are told of heroics
and of struggles unknown to others,
contemplate the void of our experience
that has left us alone, together.

We,
wending our weary way
down the tunnel of uncertainty,
catch rays and glints in the distance
impelling us to follow our instincts
to find the bridge to the beyond.

We,
together in a capsule, catapulted
away from the terrestrial sphere,
travel in terrible anguish, believing
ourselves to be anointed in despair
as we search for an identity in reality.

We,
who sometimes misunderstand each other
when we lose the art of communicating,
fumble around in search of
that elusive chemistry that has
sustained us over the fire-seared years.

We,
finding each other again amongst the broken china
are bonded in shackles of steel,
and carry our burdens with us
through tempests and calm
to emerge triumphantly alive, still together.

Me,
fighting the insidious cancer-like growth
that eats away my mind;
You,
emaciated and confused
struggling to retain a hold on life;
Together,
our destinies are inexorably entwined
as we call upon each other for succour
to go forth and challenge the odds.

SELF-PORTRAIT: MADNESS

I am the madwoman,
but I am not locked away in an attic.
Somehow I roam the world in a haze,
thinking I know what is to be known.
I soar beyond the rainbows to join
the celestial beings in a fanciful flight
which seems to unite me with the ethereal.
Perhaps I am a Visionary!

But deep inside my madness there lies a woman
who says my visions appear to no one else,
who says my voices speak to no one else,
who says I am delusional,
and with whom I wrestle for control of my psyche.

I am afraid of this sane woman
because she sees the pathos and sorrow of my madness,
and throws down the gauntlet to the voices
who wish to direct the movements of my mind.
She challenges my mind's many creations
that have led me to moments of shame.

She never sleeps.
Most of all she seeks to order the chaos,
and however fragile that order may be
the mind can be at peace with the spinning world.

SELF-PORTRAIT: SANITY

I am the sane woman,
and I am locked away in an attic
where the manners of a static world prevail.
Here life is circumscribed to a reality
which has a lifelessness of the dead
and the visionlessness of lost dreams.
Everywhere the manacles of slavery abound
and I find my mind fettered to a code of law
that regulates the moods and feelings.
Most of all there is order,
a perceptible but fragile order we all know.

But deep inside my sanity there lies a woman
who says my sanity is a sham.

I am afraid of this madwoman
because she knows the truth of my untruth.
She listens to my everyday existence
and lurks just out of sight.

She never sleeps.
She only waits to create a kind of alternative
and challenge accepted realities.
She only waits to reveal herself in a pageant
of lively characters who belong to
the fringes of the mind's liquid boundaries.

DEATH WISH

Death always seems a moment away
as I grasp at it with a vengeance.
The blackest of holes looms before me
and the desire to rest myself in Death's
cavernous coffin womb compels
me to perform one last act.

I have such a fear of life
with all its pain and anguish
that I hold out my hand to Death,
imploring it to transport me to
somewhere far away and unreachable.
I seize Death by the throat in a desperation
I find fearful and strange as I
stumble through life with my battered senses
flailing all the way — restless and numb.

I call upon you Death,
to use your magic wooing powers
and take me in your skeletal arms
on a journey to all the Gardens of Eden,
and on into a timeless zone.
Garland me with flowers of ruby
and make me beautiful at this terrible time,
because when I look into myself, I find
my within missing and I can no longer go on.

Death, you are a moment away.

LIFE WISH

Life is a celebration of being,
and with an incredible desire I hold it
firmly in my grasp, never wishing to let go—
for how fragile is this thing.

O for immortality and longevity
to witness the passage of history with
the rise and fall of civilizations;
to watch Life come and go while I remain
revitalized along the way by the gifts of Life.

I do not wish to burn in the inferno,
or give my corpse to crawling worms in the grave—
burning and rotting are not for me.

I want Life to flow through my senses
and tantalize me with the sheer delight
of existence in a world which
rewards the searcher with a kind of grace.
And I seek the mysteries of Life to
give me a knowledge of the ways.

I call upon you Life,
to use your magic wooing powers
and take me on a wondrous journey
where I can feel all your richness and beauty
infuse itself into my soul, making me
as a fragrant flower in a field.

Life, you are many moments of joy.

DESPAIR

I am alone without belief
roaming the wilderness.

I am a madwoman without relief
roaming the wilderness.

I am full of grief
roaming the wilderness.

My life will be brief.

THE RAZOR'S EDGE

Living on the razor's edge is a desperate struggle
to balance the hopeless and the ecstatic;
to separate the real from the imaginary;
to vanquish the ghosts;
to establish a clear mind where
stability resolves all the quandaries
of a double-edged life.

But acid thoughts reveal the turmoil of
my mind in a state of agony,
and the task to liberate myself
from the bewilderment before me is awesome.
A fragile entity, my mind moves
in waves of thought upon confused thought,
and is driven by the ghosts which crush the self.
My soul teeters before the dark door —
its barriers assailed
by a myriad hostile spectres.
This agony consumes the life forces
and the once calm waters become
squalls and tempests that devastate
all in their wake, leaving no one unscathed.

And sinking into the turbulent waters,
I am drowning in a sea of madness,
lashed to the mast of the sinking Ship of Fools.

I Have Seen

I have seen the best minds destroyed by madness.

I have seen them drag their drugged bodies
around hospital wards, shackled by
their ball and chain of medication.

I have seen them sitting in old chairs,
shoulders slumped, pallid faces and trembling hands,
fixated by their delusions and voices,
waiting for time to alleviate the anguish.

I have seen their fear and bewilderment
as they are escorted through the locked doors
by nurses who can only guess at
the workings of the minds they observe.

I have seen an eternity of suffering
in their hollow eyes and ghostly faces
as they search for something that eludes them.

I have seen these broken people,
with shattered personalities,
trying to piece together
the fragments of their lives
that will never be whole or united again.

I have seen their desperate struggles
for survival against a foe
that knows no boundary and has no compassion.

I have seen myself.

WHO WANTS TO KNOW

I am not afraid to claim my madness
but I would not wish it upon anyone else.
Who would want to know the ache
of the isolation of fragmentation—
not to feel whole and at home with oneself—
of having to cope with an overload of information
that storms through the disparate mind.
Who would want to spend endless days
of desperate aloneness and loneliness
with the fear that one's head is about to explode—
Who can know the feelings of one's mind
being wired with numerous electric leads,
which are plugged into the wall sockets that send
powerful jolts through one's body and mind,
creating continuous buzzing and frenetic thoughts—
Who wants to know that I wrestle
every day with veiled, turbid forces
which creep upon me when I am off guard—
Who wants to know that I am not the
only one to lose the interlacing of being—
many, many souls suffer more than I.
Still, I claim my madness and speak out
to the world at large about my world within,
and ask for compassion for our battered psyches.

THE DARK DOOR

And yet I am, and live — like vapors tossed

Into the nothingness of scorn and noise,
*   Into the living sea of waking dreams,*
Where there is neither sense of life or joys,
*   But the vast shipwreck of my life's esteems.*

John Clare

She, in lonely silence, sat
her plunging mood set soaring
down, down to the Dark Door
poised to engulf her at its entrance;
to shut tightly the gate behind her
in solemn captivity.

All year long,
the gate in brooding wait
had remained an open port,
some resisting its callings
passing by without stopping,
many, never seeing it before,
stopping in curious wonder
at why such a glorious gate
reeked of a stench so vile.

All year long,
the long drawn-out year
when time seemed to slouch its pace,
her fervent resistance took its toll
until she, in stony mood
of numb despair and doubt,
fell awkwardly from her station
into that putrid portal's realm
to hear the slamming
of the prison door behind her.
Upon her face
the cold, rancid breath of darkness'
intimations of love blew.
Upon her burning ears
fell the lusting whispers
of the demon of the depths.
And she, in lonely silence,
succumbed to the unbeckoned
giver of poisonous potions
and the turbid black bile
of black melancholy.

SPIRITUS INSANIAE

A shade, who appears
from the guts of the earth,
unable to shed the
cloying cloak of madness,
stands astride a chariot of fire
and calls me to his side.

His eyes, staring fixedly,
as though lost to some other world,
look through me like a laser
piercing an unknown realm of my soul.

Suddenly, an anguished cry
escapes his lips: *I who am distant*,
evoking the solitariness that crushes
those touched with the
abstraction of imposed folly.

I cannot dismiss this shade
whose words swell and well
in my cheerless mind,
reminding me of my own isolation.
I who am distant,
feathers my lips.

This baneful, wretched thing
that wrests sense from the mind,
is heedless of impassioned defiance.

Reluctantly, I mount the chariot,
imbued with the scourge that beset him.
We lurch forward, wheels ablaze,
on a journey to the place where
the imaginary wrestles with the real,
both of us impaled by the sword
of *Spiritus Insaniae*.

LARUNDEL: 'A' WARD 1991

In armchairs they languish
their eyes filled with anguish
in the sorrow and gloom
of the stale smoky room.

And nervous, trembling hands hold
upon their knees ashtrays old,
the butt-ends of cigarette smoke
while many drink their cans of coke.

Gazing all around they know
the dreadful, sad tales of woe,
locked away from the spinning world
with reason gone, their wings are furled.

So their minds are racked with pain
yet words alone cannot explain
how madness crushed all the goals
of these silent, joyless souls.

AND NOISE DROWNS THE BREATH
OF THE NIGHT GOING BY

Thunder cracking,
lightning bolting,
rain deluging,
no quiet here where
the elements in my head
rage in Shakespearean chaos.
The Mistral howls.
Sleep eludes heavy eyes.
Then the callings of
the unwelcome visitors
with shrill voices
and grotesque torch songs.
Gaggles of strangers parade
through my cranium's chambers
laughing like a thousand hyenas.

And noise drowns the breath
of the night going by.

Who sounds there?
I look, but no one appears,
while the bludgeoning continues
by the unrelenting noise.
I look, peering into the night
for the source of the
irrepressible shouting around me —
surely the Devil has a hand
in this cacophonous display.

I look for my accusers
whose treacherous words I hear.
I must be evil!

And noise drowns the breath
of the night going by.

Then a quiet descends.
This is no ordinary quiet.
Furtive whisperers brush my senses
with breezy words that filter,
sinister-like, through the
low-lying troughs of my mind.
Peace is far away.
My life-force reels.
The phantoms bring a disquiet.
The tumult seethes.
There is more noise from
these capricious whisperers
than the boisterous twangs
of a bank of electric guitars.

And noise drowns the breath
of the night going by.

RESTLESSNESS

Like a reeling pendulum
cutting its way through the air,
up and down, back and forth,
so I reel too, unbearably restless,
pacing the path like a caged lioness,
my feet — untrammelled
a thirst — unquenchable
a desire — insatiable.
Unable to rein in my mind,
my supplicating soul seeks
a divine message
and rest, sweet rest,
eternal rest.

DEATH RISING

I

When day succumbs
to the nightly shroud
and I rest my head
upon a beckoning pillow,
body racked from the day's demands —
not physical, but the ever repetitious
banging of my head against the gate
that keeps me from that longed for place —
how tired my self is,
how utterly spent I feel
with the mental pain that
throbs and throbs and throbs
and throws back my head
with anguish that never relents.

II

Into the night I slide
asking favours of the morrow.

III

The call of the morning
with the lifting of the shroud
awakens the birds,
stirs the day
and summons the sleepers
from their pillows.
The dead come to life
standing before mirrors
to see themselves risen,
but I —
I gaze into the mirror
and see a dead person.
I do not rise like the rest.
I wake to death.
I am death peering at death.
Through the night's slumber
the dark shroud had failed to lift.
Death clasps my hand
like a terrifying friend,
inducting me into his realm,
leading me into that nothing place

where all I feel is the weight of the grave
and the sadness of absence,
and all those things that held me together
are riven from my vacuous soul.
Feeling like a ghost who sees
yet is unseen,
walking numb and cold
without breath or pulse,
a stiffened corpse
untouched by the teeming streets
or splendid bucolic scenes,
I dwell in life as deep death.

WHITE LIGHT/ WHITE MADNESS

Standing in the afternoon sun
lost and nowhere to go,
42 degree heat
10 per cent humidity
north wind gusting to 70 km/h
a perilous day of Total Fire Ban
everything gasping for air
everything parched to dust;
standing in this furnace
naked, bare and blistered
squinting eyes blinded
by relentless, burning heat
and rays of light
brighter than a thousand suns,
I stand alone, defenceless.

Assailed by shaft after shaft
of searing, spearing, scorching,
blazing, white, white light,
piercing with the power of a laser,
penetrating my cranium-shell,
bombarding the neurones
with blinding, blistering flashes
melting my senses
seizing up my thoughts-engine,
my mind gasps for cool sanity
trying desperately to deflect
the tendril white light waves
of white madness.

HELLO? IS ANYONE OUT THERE?

With a little help from my friends.

Thank you for calling Crisis Line Inc.
We provide a service to help you streamline your breakdown.
Press 1 to continue.
Press 2 to quit.

If you are having a minor breakdown our service is not
designed for you.
Press 1 and quit.
If you are having a major breakdown
Press 2.

If you have private health insurance
Press 1 and speak to a counsellor immediately.
If you do not have private health insurance
Press 2.

To continue your call, please enter your Medicare number,
followed by the # key.
Please enter the 4 digit expiry date on your Medicare card,
followed by the * key.
Press 1 to continue.

Your number is 21037 15643 57498 18326 42695 00063 3
Expiry date 05/02.
If this is correct
Press 1.
If this is incorrect
Press 2 and start again.
If you are totally confused
Press 3 to quit.

If you have a diagnosis of Schizophrenia
Press 1.
If you have a diagnosis of Bipolar Disorder
Press 2.
If you have a diagnosis of Depression
Press 3.
If you have a diagnosis of Borderline Personality Disorder
Press 4 and quit.
If you have no particular diagnosis
Press 5 and quit.
If you are just a little sad and lonely
Press 6 and quit.
If you are questioning your sexuality
Press 7 and quit.
If you are having an existential crisis
Press 8 and quit.

Thank you for accessing our Schizophrenia Line
Press 1 to continue.
Press 2 to quit.
If you are hearing voices
Press 1.
If you are having visions of the Virgin Mary
Press 2.
If you think you are Joan of Arc
Press 3.
If you are getting messages from the television
Press 4.
If you are having paranoid thoughts and think you are linked into
an intergalactic computer
Press 5.
If you think there is a world conspiracy to exterminate you
Press 6.

If you think we can help you, you are obviously delusional
Press 7 for a prescription for antipsychotic medication.
Press 8 for hospitalisation procedures.
Press 9 to quit.

If you are seriously suicidal
Press 1.
If you are merely attention seeking
Press 2 and quit.

If you would like to hear this message again
Press 3.

Sorry, the computer cannot confirm your call.
Sorry, the computer cannot confirm your call.
Sorry, the computer cannot confirm your call.

If you are dead, please have your partner press 1 to quit.

Thank you for accessing our service.
Your receipt number is 5998 6634 7006

If you do not call again within the next 24 hours, you may be
eligible for 20,000 Frequent Flyer points. Do take advantage of this
once in a lifetime offer.

Have a nice day.

A THESAURUS OF MADNESS

for Margaret

(People Must Think I'm Crazy)

Being the madwoman, I am also: a lunatic, a maddy, a mental case, a bedlamite, a screwball, a nut, a loon, a loony, a madcap, a mad dog, a psychopath, a maniac, an hysteric, a psychotic, a manic depressive, a megalomaniac, a pyromaniac, a kleptomaniac, a crackpot, an eccentric, an oddity, an idiot, a basket case, demented, moon-struck, hazy, unhinged, dippy, loopy, distracted, pixy-led, a scatterbrain, certifiable, crazy, loco, psycho, a nutter, possessed, fevered, bonkers, obsessed, bedevilled, troppo, starkers, schizo, potty, nuts, daft, dilly, a crackbrain, a fruit-cake, touched.

Being insane, I suffer from: mental illness, psychiatric illness, brain damage, unsoundness of mind, alienation, lunacy, madness, mental derangement, mental instability, abnormal psychology, loss of reason, intellectual unbalance, mental decay, a darkened mind, a troubled brain, a deranged intellect, nerves, imbecility, cretinism, morosis, feeblemindedness, queerness, having a screw loose, bats in the belfry, rats in the upper storey, nervous breakdowns.

Being as I am, mad that is, I must be: bananas, crackers, a camel short of a caravan, a ball short of an over, a pad short of a kit, not in my right mind, bereft of reason, deprived of my wits, as mad as a snake, a tinnie short of a slab, diseased in the mind, as mad as a hatter, wildered in my wits, not the full quid, a brick short of a load, off my rocker, round the bend, a candidate for Bedlam, foaming at the mouth, as mad as meat axe, up the pole, a sandwich short of a picnic, out of my tree, off my face, off my block, over the edge, off my saucer, a shilling short of a pound, as silly as a wheel, off my trolley, as mad as a two-bob watch, a shingle short and I have a kangaroo loose in the top paddock.

Being wild and distraught, I live in: a madhouse, a mental home, a mental hospital, an asylum, a lunatic asylum, an insane asylum, Bedlam, a booby hatch, a loony-bin, a nut house, a bug house, a psychiatric hospital, the rat house, the giggle factory, the rat factory, the funny farm.

> I am many things, in many places.
> Fool that I may be, mad that I may be.
> I am, in all my precarious guises,
> the creation of a cruel mind.

ACKNOWLEDGEMENTS

Some of the poems in this collection have been previously published in the following anthologies: *Difference* (1985), **The Exploding Frangipani** (1990) and *Noses Earthward* (1997).

Some have appeared in the following magazines: *Tirra Lirra, Social Alternatives* and *Art Streams*.

Several were published as part of the Poems on Trams Project.

OTHER POETRY TITLES FROM SPINIFEX PRESS

Sandy Jeffs
Blood Relations

Bearing witness was unbearable — Sandy Jeffs

Sandy Jeffs' poems inhabit the darkness at the heart of the dysfunctional family. The ravaged emotionality of these poems will speak to anyone who has felt its pain.
— Doris Brett

… a courageous and powerful journey … Sandy Jeffs explores the dynamics including the secrecy, the unspeakable effects on the children, and the healing. — Patricia Easteal

These poems speak with confronting directness of family lives deeply scarred by love distorted, by raging violence, alcohol, madness. It is as if only a language 'scoured' of artifice and sentimentality can encompass such experiences of Blood Relations, and chart the complex and fluctuating reactions of bewilderment, anger, guilt and compassion that mark indelibly these memoirs of a survivor. — Jennifer Strauss

ISBN 1 875559 98 1

Patricia Sykes
Wire Dancing

Circus as drama and risk, as exuberance and irrepressible spirit, is the central metaphor Patricia Sykes uses to open a world where private and public share the same tightrope. The poems speak of women searching for footholds along the spectrums of politics, power, history, culture and relationships. *Theirs are performances drawing on the blood of sugars of language* and *the cinemascopes of hope* as they wire dance through circumcision and incest, madness and suicide, genocide and war. There is passion and resistance, *hot comedy* and *fire in the belly*. *Falling is the first victory*, balance is the ultimate skill.

… passionate, witty, erudite and ironic … the poetry experience of the year. — Bev Roberts

ISBN 1 875559 90 6

Susan Hawthorne
Bird

Birds don't fly with leads, I said.
Safety belts are to learn with, not to live with—
I'm safer on the trapeze than crossing the road.
And I do that every day, often by myself.

So thirteen-year-old Avis argues when confronted by the limitations imposed on her at school.

Many-eyed and many-lived is this poet … To the classic figures of Sappho and Eurydice she brings all the Now! Here! sense of discovery that fires her modern girl taking lessons in flight. — Judith Rodriguez

ISBN 1 875559 88 4

Lizz Murphy
Two Lips Went Shopping

Two Lips Went Shopping is a book for anyone who has
ever shopped—or worked in shops. But whether you find
yourself wincing or laughing could depend on which side
of the shop counter you're on at the time.

Find out what it's like to be a young shopgirl, vent your
frustrations with today's supermarket society and the
advertising and media industries, take a nostalgic trip
back to the days of the corner shop.

Using consumerism as a platform, *Two Lips Went
Shopping* gives insights to world issues including the baby
trade, Female Genital Mutilation and women in war and
protest.

ISBN 1 875559 96 5

Robyn Rowland
Perverse Serenity

What happens when an Australian feminist falls in love
with an Irish monk? Daring, passionate and forceful
poetry about the limits of love and obsession.

*Here is writing not afraid to be vulnerable, not trapped in
literary artifice, not reticent about emotion, its hopes, its
fears, its withdrawals and assertions, which we all share and
which enrich our humanity.* — Barret Reid

ISBN 1 875559 13 2

Merlinda Bobis
Summer was a Fast Train
without Terminals

An epic of the old Philippines, lyric reflections on longing, and an erotic dance drama make up this fine collection.

Bobis can produce some genuinely haunting pieces. This is a touching work from an established poet. — Hamesh Wyatt, *Otago Daily Times*, NZ

ISBN 1 875559 76 0

Gillian Hanscombe
Sybil: The Glide of Her Tongue

A book where the lesbian voice meditates the essential vitality of she-dykes who have visions. A book where Gillian Hanscombe's poetry opens up meaning in such a way that it provides for beauty and awareness, for a space where one says yes to a lesbian we of awareness. — Nicole Brossard

O I am enamoured of Sybil. Gillian Hanscombe is one of the most insightfully ironic, deliciously lyrical voices we have writing amongst us today. — Betsy Warland

ISBN 1 875559 05 1

Suniti Namjoshi
Feminist Fables

An ingenious reworking of fairytales. Mythology mixed
with the author's original material and vivid
imagination. An indispensable feminist classic.

*Her imagination soars to breathtaking heights ... she has the
enviable skill of writing stories that are as entertaining as they
are thought-provoking.* — Kerry Lyon, Australian Book
Review

ISBN 1 875559 19 1

Suniti Namjoshi
St Suniti and the Dragon

Ironic and fantastic, elegant and elegaic, fearful and
funny. A thoroughly modern fable.

*I can think of plenty of adjectives to describe St Suniti and the
Dragon, but not a noun to go with them. It's hilarious, witty,
elegantly written, hugely inventive, fantastic, energetic ...
With work as original as this, it's easier to fling words at it
than to say what it is or what it does.* — U.A. Fanthorpe

ISBN 1 875559 18 3

Louise Crisp
Ruby Camp

Crisp's insights and perceptions are so original and intense that she has needed to find a new language, precise and sensuous, mysterious and revealing, held in a fine balance of rhythm and phrasing. She creates a radically new way of 'knowing' the East Gippsland bush: 'strong as illusion the dream works/ its way into landscape'. It is finally a book about joy. — Marie Tulip

Miriel Lenore
Travelling Alone Together

Three journeys across the Nullarbor and time are interwoven as Lenore explores our myths.

This poet/traveller is incredibly modest and respectful of what is given her to experience. She travels across her many landscapes naming without appropriating. — Alison Clark

ISBN 1 875559 83 3

Diane Fahey
The Body in Time

Diane Fahey pieces together a world — with integrity and incomparable delicacy — much as the fragile light of a star defines a universe. — Annie Greet

Jordie Albiston
Nervous Arcs

Jordie Albiston writes with sharp intelligence, lyrical grace, and moral passion. A name to watch for. — Janette Turner Hospital

Winner, Mary Gilmore Award, 1996
Second Prize, Anne Elder FAW Award, 1996

ISBN 1 875559 37 X

If you would like to know more about Spinifex Press
write for a free catalogue or visit our website –

SPINIFEX PRESS
PO Box 212 North Melbourne
Victoria 3051 Australia
http://www.spinifexpress.com.au